MIMESIS INTERN

PHILOSOPHY
n. 6

QUENTIN MEILLASSOUX

TIME WITHOUT BECOMING

Edited by Anna Longo

MIMESIS
INTERNATIONAL

© 2014 – Mimesis International
www.mimesisinternational.com
e-mail: info@mimesisinternational.com

Book series: *Philosophy*, n. 6

Isbn 9788857523866

© MIM Edizioni Srl
P.I. C.F. 0241937030

CONTENTS

QUENTIN MEILLASSOUX

TIME WITHOUT
BECOMING

TIME WITHOUT BECOMING[1]

I would like, first of all, to say that I'm very happy to have the opportunity to discuss my work here at Middlesex University, and I'd like to express my thanks to the organizers of this conference, especially to Peter Hallward and Ray Brassier.

I am going to expound and set out the fundamental decisions of *After Finitude*, specifically concerning the two fundamental notions I tried to elaborate in this book: that of "correlationism" and that of "the principle of factiality".

1. *Correlationism*

I call "correlationism" the contemporary opponent of any realism. Correlationism takes many contemporary forms, but particularly those of transcendental philosophy, the varieties of phenomenology, and post-modernism. But although these currents are all extraordinarily varied in themselves, they all share, according to me, a more or less explicit decision: that there are no objects, no events, no laws, no beings which are not always already correlated with a point of view, with a subjective access. Anyone maintaining the contrary, i.e. that it is possible to attain something like a reality in itself, existing absolutely independently of his viewpoint, or his categories, or his epoch, or his culture, or his language, etc., this person would be exemplarily naïve, or if you prefer: a realist,

---

1   "Time without becoming" is the text of the talk that Quentin Meillassoux gave at the Middlesex University, London, 8 May 2008.

a metaphysician, a quaintly dogmatic philosopher. With the term of "correlationism", I wanted to set out the basic argument of these "philosophies of access" – to use Graham Harman's expression – but also – and I insist on this point – the exceptional strength of its antirealist argumentation, which is apparently so desperately implacable. Correlationism rests on an argument as simple as powerful, and which can be formulated in this way: there can be no X without a givenness of X, and no theory about X without a positing of X. If you speak about something, the correlationist will say, you speak about something that is given to you, and posited by you. The argument for this thesis is as simple to formulate as it is difficult to refute: it can be called the "argument from the circle", and consists in remarking that every objection against correlationism is an objection produced by your thinking, and so dependent upon it. When you speak against correlation, you forget that you speak against correlation, hence from the viewpoint of your own mind, or culture, or epoch, etc. The circle means that there is a vicious circle in any naïve realism, a performative contradiction through which you refute what you say or think by your very act of saying it or thinking it.

I think there are two principal versions of correlationism: a transcendental one, which claims that there are some universal forms of the subjective knowledge of things, and the post-modern one, which denies the existence of any such subjective universality. But in both cases there is a denial of an absolute knowledge – I mean a knowledge of the thing in itself independently of our subjective access to it. Consequently, for correlationists the sentence "X is", means "X is the correlate of thinking" – thinking in the Cartesian sense – that is: X is the correlate of an affection, or a perception, or a conception, or of any other subjective or intersubjective act. To be is to be a correlate, the term of a correlation. And when you claim to think any specific X, you must posit this X, which you cannot separate from this specific act of positing. This is why it is impossible to conceive an absolute X, i.e.

an X which would be essentially separate from a subject. We can't know what reality is in itself because we can't distinguish between those properties which are supposed to belong to the object, and those properties belonging to the subjective access to the object. Of course concrete correlationisms are far more complex than my model: but I maintain that this model is the minimal decision of any anti-realism. And because this is the very decision I want to contest, I don't need here to go into the details of specific and historical philosophies. Of course, it would take too long to examine here the precise relations between correlationism, considered as the contemporary model of anti-realism, and the complex history of the critiques of dogmatism in modern philosophy. But we can say that the "argument from the circle" means not only that the thing in itself is unknowable, as in Kant, but that the in itself is radically unthinkable. Kant, as you know, said that it was impossible to know the thing in itself, but he granted to theoretical reason – leaving practical reason aside here – the capacity to access four determinations of the in itself. According to Kant, I know 1) that the thing in itself effectively exists outside of consciousness (there are not only phenomena); 2) we know that it affects our sensibility and produces in us representations (that's why our sensibility is passive, finite, and not spontaneous); 3) the thing in itself is not contradictory – the principle of non-contradiction is an absolute principle, not one that is merely relative to our consciousness; 4) and, lastly, we know that the thing in itself can't be spatiotemporal because space and time can only be forms of subjective sensibility and not properties of the in itself: in other words, we don't know what the thing in itself is, but we know absolutely what it is not. So, as you can see, Kant is rather "loquacious" about the thing in itself, and as you know, post-Kantian speculation had destroyed such claims by denying even the possibility of an in itself outside the self. But contemporary correlationism is not a speculative idealism: it doesn't say dogmatically that there is no in itself, but only that we can't say anything about it, not even that it exists – and that's precisely why, according to me, the term "in itself" has disappeared from these discourses. Thought only has to deal with a world correlated with itself, and with the inconceivable fact of the being of such a correlation. That there is a thought-world correlation thought is the supreme enigma which gives by contrast the possibility of an utterly different situation. The *Tractatus Logico-Philosophicus*[2] is a good example of such a discourse, when it designates as "mystical" the mere fact that there is a consistent world; a logical, non-contradictory world.

2. *The problem of the arche-fossil*

My goal is very simple: I attempt to refute every form of correlationism – which is to say that I try to demonstrate that thinking, under very special conditions, can access reality as it is in itself, independently of any act of subjectivity. In other words, I maintain that an absolute, i.e. a reality absolutely separate from the subject, can be thought by the subject. This is apparently a contradiction, and, at first glance, exactly what a naïve realist would maintain. My challenge is to demonstrate that it can be a non-contradictory proposition, and one that is non-naïve, but speculative. So I must explain two things about this assertion: first, why do I think it is imperative that we break with correlationism? In order to explain this point, I will set out a specific problem that I call the "problem of *ancestrality*". Secondly, I must explain how we can refute the supposedly implacable argument of the correlational circle. For this purpose, I will expound a speculative principle that I call the *principle of factiality* ("principe de factualité" en français).

Let's begin with the first point. Correlationism, according to me, comes up against a serious problem, which I call the

---

2   Ludwig Wittgenstein, *Tractatus Logico-philosophicus*, London: Routledge 1974.

"problem of the *arche-fossil*", or the "problem of a*ncestral-ity*". A fossil is a material bearing traces of pre-historic life: but what I call an "arche-fossil" is a material indicating traces of "ancestral" phenomena anterior even to the emergence of life. I call "ancestral" a reality – a thing or an event – which existed before life on earth. Science is now able to produce statements (let's say: "ancestral statements") describing ancestral realities thanks to the radioactive isotope, whose rate of decay provides an index of the age of rock samples, or thanks to the starlight whose luminescence provides an index of the age of distant stars. Science can, in this way, produce statements, such as: that the universe is roughly 14 billion years old, or that the Earth formed roughly 4.5 billion years ago. So my question is very straightforward. I simply ask: what are the conditions of possibility of ancestral statements? This is a question formulated in a transcendental style, it has transcendental allure, so to speak, but my point is that it is impossible to answer this question by means of Critical philosophy. My question, indeed, is more precise: I ask if correlationism – in any of its versions – is able to give a sense, or a meaning to ancestral statements. And what I try to show is that it is impossible for correlationism, in spite of all the various forms of subtle argumentations it is able to invent, it is impossible, I maintain, for correlationism to give sense to natural science's capacity to produce ancestral statements thanks to the arche-fossils (radioactive isotope, stellar luminescence). How could one give sense to the idea of a time preceding the subject, or consciousness or *Dasein*, a time within which subjectivity or *being-in-the-world* itself emerged, and which perhaps will disappear along with humanity and terrestrial life, if one makes of time, and space, and the visible world, the strict correlates of this subjectivity? If time is a correlate of the subject, then nothing can actually precede the subject – as individual or more radically as human species – inside time. Because what existed before the subject existed before the subject *for* the subject. Appeals to intersubjectivity are of no account here, since the time in question is not the time preceding such or such an individual – this time is still social, made up of the subjective temporality of ancestors – but a time preceding all life, and so every human community. I maintain that there are an infinity of ways in which the different versions of correlationism can try to deny or mask this *aporia* and I tried to deconstruct some of these in *After Finitude*[3]. But this denial follows from a certitude: that there can be no realist or materialist solution to the problem of ancestrality. But I maintain that such a solution exists: that's why I'm able to see and state the obvious: correlationism can't give any sense to ancestral statements and, consequently, to a science which is able to produce such statements. Science is reduced to an explanation of the world given-to-a-subject. Of course, I also know that transcendental philosophy or phenomenology is always said to be essentially distinct from crude idealism of the Berkeleyian variety. But what I try to demonstrate in *After Finitude* is that every correlationism collapses into this crude idealism when it has to think the significance of ancestrality.

Why did I choose the term "correlationism" rather than a well known term like "idealism" to designate my intellectual adversary? Because I wanted to disqualify the usual retort used by transcendental philosophy and phenomenology against the accusation of idealism, responses such as "Kantian critique is not a subjective idealism since there is a refutation of idealism in the *Critique of Pure Reason*", or "Phenomenology is not a dogmatic idealism, since intentionality is oriented towards a radical exteriority, and it is not a solipsism since the givenness of the object implies according to Husserl the reference to an intersubjective community". And the same could be said of *Dasein* as the originary "being-in-the world". Even though these positions claim that they are not subjective idealisms, they can't deny, at the risk of self-refutation, that the exteriority which they elaborated is essentially relative: relative to a consciousness, a language, a Dasein, etc. Consequently all that correlationism can say about ancestrality is that it is

---

3   Quentin Meillassoux, *After Finitude: Essay on the Necessity of Contingency*, London: Continuum 2008.

a subjective representation of such a past, but that this past couldn't really have existed in itself with all its objects and events. Correlationism will generally maintain – because it is subtle – that ancestral statements are true in a way, i.e. as universal statements, bearing on some present experiences about specific materials (starlight, isotope), or at least as a statement accepted by the present community of scientists. But if it is consistent, correlationism will have to deny that the referents of these statements really existed as described prior to any human or living species. For the correlationist, ancestrality cannot be a reality prior to the subjects, but a reality said and thought *by* the subject as prior to the subject. It is a past for humanity which has no more effectiveness than that of a past of humanity that is strictly correlated with actual humans. But this assertion is, of course, a catastrophe, because it destroys the sense of scientific statements, which, I insist, just mean what they mean. An ancestral and scientific statement doesn't say that something existed before subjectivity *for* subjectivity, but that something existed before subjectivity, and nothing more than this: the ancestral statement has a realistic meaning, or it has no meaning at all. Because to say that something existed before you just for you, just on condition that you exist to be conscious of this past, it is to say that nothing existed before you. It is to say the contrary of what ancestrality means: that reality in itself existed independently of your perception of it as your own past. Your past is your past, only if it has effectively been a present without you, not only a present thought presently as a past. Such a past is not a past, whatever you can say, but an illusion produced by a sort of retrojection, a past produced now as a past absolutely preceding the present.

As you know, Kant, following Diderot[4], considered it a scandal for philosophy that a proof of the existence of things

---

4   D. Diderot, "Letter on the Blind For the Use of Those Who See", in *Diderot's early philosophical works*, London and Chicago: Open Court 1916, p. 68.

outside the subject had not yet been established[5]. Couldn't
I be accused of resurrecting this old problem, which is generally considered as outdated? Heidegger, in *Sein und Zeit*,
famously inverted the Kantian proposition saying that the
scandal was rather that this sort of proof was still attempted
and awaited[6]. This assertion is explained by the very structure of phenomenological subjectivity: in Husserl's intentionality, in Heidegger's *being-in-the-world*, or in Sartre's
"éclatement" towards the "chose même", far from being a
superfluously added element of an intrinsically solipsistic
subject, the outside is an originary structure of the subject,
rendering any attempted proof of an external reality obsolete and rather ridiculous. Still, I said, the question persists,
even after phenomenology, and even within phenomenology.
Although phenomenologists can say that consciousness is
originally correlated and open to a world, what can they say
about a pre-human and pre-animal reality, about ancestrality, this domain of non-correlation as lacking any subject?
How are the sciences able to speak so precisely about this
domain, if this domain is no more than a retrospective illusion? What would nature without us be? What would remain in it if we were not there anymore? This question is
so far from obsolete for phenomenology, that it became a
great question for Heidegger himself in the thirties. He wrote
to Elisabeth Blochmann on 11th October 1931: "I often ask
myself – this has for a long time been a fundamental question for me – what nature would be without man, must it
not resonate through him (*hindurschwingen*) in order to attain its own most potency?". In this letter we discover that
Heidegger himself is unable to renounce to this question and
that his own attempt at answering it, is both enigmatic and
probably inspired of Schellingian metaphysics, as suggests
the term "potency" *(Macht, oder Potenz)*. We see here how

---

5   I. Kant, *The Critic of Pure Reason*, Introduction to the second
     edition, B XXXIX.
6   M. Heidegger, *Being and Time*, London: SCM Press, 1962, §43.

far Heidegger was from being able to disqualify or resolve the question of ancestrality: what is nature without man, and how can we think the time in which nature has produced the subject, or *Dasein*?

But you must understand the exact significance of this problem of ancestrality in my strategy.

What is very important for me is that I don't pretend to refute correlationism by means of ancestrality: the problem of ancestrality is not – at all – intended as a refutation of correlationisme, this would be naïve. In fact, in the first chapter of *After Finitude*, I simply try to lay out an *aporia*, rather than a refutation. That is, on the one hand it seems impossible to think via correlationism the ability of natural sciences to produce ancestral statements; but on the other hand, it seems impossible to refute the correlationist position, because it seems impossible to maintain that we could be able to know what there is when we are not. How could we imagine the existence of color without an eye to see it or the existence of a sound without an ear to hear it? How can we think the meaning of time or space without a subject being conscious of past, present and future, or being conscious of the difference between left and right? And first of all, how could we know this, since we are unable to see what the world looks like when there is nobody to perceive it?

On one hand, it seems impossible to refute the argument of the correlational circle, in other words, to forget that when we think something, it is we who do think something; on the other hand, it seems impossible to have a correlationist understanding of the natural sciences. Through this apparently simple, indeed even naïve problem, I pose in fact the question of philosophical naïvety: that is, the question of what exactly means "to be naïve" in philosophy. Naïvety in philosophy nowadays assumes a favored form: the belief in the possible correspondence between thinking and being – but a being that is posited precisely as independent of thinking. The entire effort of modern philosophy was to do without the concept of truth, or, according to me, and more interestingly, to fundamentally redefine this concept, replacing truth as adequation with truth considered as legality (Kant), or intersubjectivity (Husserl), or interpretation (hermeneutics). But what I try to show in *After Finitude* is that there is in ancestrality a strange resistance to every anti-adequation model. Yet this resistance doesn't directly concern the truth of scientific theories, but rather their meaning.

Let's explain this point. We certainly can't believe ingenuously that a scientific theory, I mean in the field of natural sciences, could be something like "true". Not because of some radical skepticism towards the sciences, but rather by virtue of the very process of science. In the course of its history, this process showed an extraordinary intenvetiveness in ceaselessly destroying its own theories, including the most fundamental ones, replacing them with paradigms whose novelty was so extreme that nobody could anticipate the beginning of their configuration. The same of course holds for current theories, and especially cosmological ones: we just can't say what future theories of cosmology, future theories of ancestrality, will be – the past, as one say, in unpredictable. But even if we can't positively assert that an ancestral theory is effectively true, we must maintain, I insist, that it could be true: we can't know if these theories will retain their truth in the future, but it is a possibility we can't exclude, because it is a condition of the meaning of such theories. Truth, and truth considered as something like a correspondance with reality, is a condition of meaning of theories, as hypotheses one can prefer to other ones. If one tries to dispense with the notion of truth and correspondence in attempting to understand these theories, one quickly generates entertaining absurdities. For example, if you say that ancestral truth must be defined by intersubjectivity rather than by the restitution of a pre-human reality, you must say something like: there has never existed anything like a universe preceding humanity with such and such determinations that we could effectively know – this is just nonsense – but only an agreement between scientists which legitimates the theory in question.

One maintains in the same sentence that scientists have solid reasons for accepting a theory, and that this theory describes an object – the field of pre-terrestrial life – which can't exist as described, because it is a nonsense. We have here a sort of return of the Lacanian real: the impossible for the contemporary philosopher is the realism, or correspondence. But realism seems to be the condition of sense for ancestral theories (in fact, I believe it is the condition for every scientific theory, but I can't demonstrate this here). That's why the idea of naïvety has changed: we can no longer be sure that the rejection of correspondence is not itself a naïve notion. The dogmatism of anti-adequation has become as problematic as the old pre-Kantian dogmatism. But the real difficulty is that it is also impossible, according to me, to go back to the old metaphysical concept of adequation, or to the naïve realism that analytical philosophy sometimes seems to perpetuate. We need to redefine correspondence, to find a very different concept of adequation, if we are serious about rejecting correlationism in all its power. Because, as we shall see, what we will discover outside the correlation is very different from the naïve concepts of things, properties and relations. It is a reality very different from given reality. That's why, ultimately, I prefer to describe my philosophy as a speculative materialism, rather than as a realism: because I remember the sentence of Foucault, who once said: "I am materialist, because I don't believe in reality".

So what we have here, according to me, is a powerful *aporia*: the *aporia* of the correlation versus the arche-fossil. It is this aporia I try to resolve in *After Finitude*: and my strategy for resolving it consists in effectively refuting correlationism and elaborating a new sort of scientific materialism grounded on a principle that I call the "principle of factiality". So let's now see what this principle means, and why it is able, according to me, to do what correlationism says is impossible: to know what there is when we are not.

3. *The principle of factiality*

The main problem I try to confront in *After Finitude* consists precisely in developing a materialism capable of deci-
sively refuting the correlational circle, in its simplest form,
which is also the form that is most difficult to rebut: that
is, the argument which demonstrates we can't speak against
correlation except from within correlation. Here is my strategy: the weakness of correlationism consists in the duality of
what it opposes. Strictly speaking, correlationism, as I define
it, is not an anti-realism but an anti-absolutism. Correlationism is the modern way of rejecting all possible knowledge of
an absolute: it is the claim that we are locked up in our representations – conscious, linguistic, historical ones – without
any sure means of access to an eternal reality independent of
our specific point of view. But there are two main forms of
the absolute: the realist one, which is that of a non-thinking
reality independent of our access to it, and the idealist one,
which consists on the contrary in the absolutisation of the
correlation itself. Therefore, correlationism must also refute
speculative idealism – or any form of vitalism or panpsy-
chism – if it wants to reject all modalities of the absolute.
But for this second refutation, the argument of the circle is
useless, because idealism and vitalism consist precisely in
claiming that it is the subjective circle itself which is the
absolute.

Let's examine briefly these idealist and vitalist arguments.
I call subjectivist metaphysics any absolutisation of a determinate human access to the world – and I call "subjectivist"
(for short) the supporter of any form of subjective metaphysics. The correlation between thought and being takes many
different forms: the subjectivist claims that some of these
relations – or indeed all – are determinations not only of humans or of the living, but of Being itself. The subjectivist
projects a correlation into the things themselves – it may take
the form of perception, intellection, wanting, etc. – and turns
it into the absolute. Of course, this process is far more elabo-

rate than I can show here, especially with Hegel. But the basic principle of subjectivism is always the same. It consists in refuting realism and correlationism through the following reasoning: since we cannot conceive of a being which would not be constituted by our relation to the world, since we cannot escape from the circle of correlation, the whole of these relations, or an eminent part of this whole, represents the very essence of any reality. According to the subjectivist, it is absurd to suppose, as the correlationist does, that there could be an in itself different from any human correlations with the world. The subjectivist thereby turns the argument of the circle against the correlationist himself: since we can't think any reality independent of human correlations, this means, according to him, that the supposition of such a reality existing outside the circle is non-sense. Thus the absolute is the circle itself, or at least a part of it. The absolute is thinking, or perception, or wanting, etc.: *idea*, *logos*, *Geist* (Mind), *Wille zur Macht* (Will to Power), the Bergsonian intuition of duration, etc.

This second form of absolutism reveals why it is necessary for correlationism to produce a second argument capable of responding to the idealist absolute. This necessity for a second argument is extremely important, since, as we shall see, it will become the weak-spot in the circle-fortress. This second argument is what I described in *After Finitude* as the argument from facticity, and I must now explain what it means more precisely.

I call "facticity" the absence of reason for any reality; in other words, the impossibility of providing an ultimate ground for the existence of any being. We can only attain conditional necessity, never absolute necessity. If definite causes and physical laws are posited, then we can claim that a determined effect must follow. But we shall never find a ground for these laws and causes, except eventually other ungrounded causes and laws: there is no ultimate cause, nor ultimate law, that is to say, a cause or a law including the ground of its own existence. But this facticity is also proper to thought. The Cartesian Cogito clearly shows this point. What is necessary, in the Cogito, is a conditional necessity: if I think, then I must be. But it is not an absolute necessity: it is not necessary that I should think. From the inside of the subjective correlation, I accede to my own facticity, and so to the facticity of the world correlated with my subjective access to it. I do it by attaining the lack of an ultimate reason, of a *causa sui*, able to ground my existence.

Facticity so defined is according to me the fundamental answer to any absolutisation of the correlation: for if correlation is factual, we can no longer maintain, as does the subjectivist, that it is a necessary component of every reality. Of course, an idealist might object that any attempt to conceive of the non-being of a subjective correlation results in a performative contradiction, since the very conception of it proves is that we effectively exist as a subject. But the correlationist replies that there can be no dogmatic proof that the correlation must exist rather than not, hence, this absence of necessity suffices to reject the idealist's claim of its absolute necessity. And the fact that I can't imagine the non-existence of subjectivity, since to imagine is to exist as a subject, does not prove it is impossible: I can't imagine what it is like to be dead, since to imagine it means we are still alive, but, unfortunately, this fact does not prove that death is impossible. The limits of my imagination are not the index of my immortality. But we must be careful. The correlationist doesn't claim that subjectivity must perish: maybe it is eternal as an absolute, as *Geist* or *Wille*, if not as an individual. The correlationist simply claims that we can't decide one way or the other about this hypothesis: we can't reach any eternal truth, whether realistic or idealistic. We don't know anything about the outside of the circle, not even if there is one – against realism – just as we don't know whether the circle itself is either necessary or contingent – against subjectivism. Correlationism is then composed of two arguments: the argument from the circle of correlation against naïve realism (let's use this term to describe any realism that is unable to refute the circle); and the argument from facticity, against speculative idealism. The subjectivist claimed erroneously that he could defeat the correlationist by the absolutizing correlation; I believe that we can only defeat the latter by absolutizing facticity. Let's see why.

The correlationist must maintain, against the subjectivist, that we can conceive the contingency of the correlation: that is, its possible disappearance for example, with the extinction of humanity. But, by doing so, and this is the essential point, the correlationist must admit that we can positively think of a possibility which is essentially independent of the correlation, since this is precisely the possibility of the correlation's non-being. To understand this point, we can once more consider the analogy with death: to think of myself as a mortal, I must admit that death doesn't depend on my own thinking about death. Otherwise, I would be able to disappear only on one condition: that I remain alive to think of my disappearance, and turn this event into a correlate of my access to it. In other words, I could be dying indefinitely, but I could never pass away. If the facticity of the correlation can be conceived of, if it is a notion that we can effectively conceive of – and, as we saw, this must be the case for the correlationist if he wants to refute the subjectivist – then it is a notion that we can think as an absolute: the absolute absence of reason for any reality, in other words, the effective ability for every determined entity, whether it is an event, a thing, or a law, to appear and disappear with no reason for its being or non-being. Unreason becomes the attribute of an absolute time capable of destroying or creating any determinate entity without any reason for its creation or destruction.

Through this thesis, I try to reveal the condition for the thinkability of the fundamental opposition in correlationism, even when this opposition is not stated or is denied: this is the opposition of the in itself and the for-us. The thesis of the correlationist, whether explicitly stated or not, is that I can't know what reality would be without me. According to him, if I remove myself from the world, I can't know the residue.

But this reasoning assumes that we enjoy positive access to an absolute possibility: the possibility that the in itself could be different from the for-us. And this absolute possibility is grounded in turn upon the absolute facticity of the correlation. It is because I can conceive of the non-being of the correlation, that I can conceive the possibility of the in it-self being essentially different from the world correlated with human subjectivity. It is because I can conceive of the absolute facticity of everything, that I can be skeptical towards every other kind of absolute. Consequently, according to me, it is possible to refute the correlationist refutation of realism – which is based upon the accusation of performative contradiction – as I discover a performative contradiction in the correlationist's reasoning. In fact, its fundamental notions, the for-us and the in it-self, are grounded on an implicit absolutization: the absolutization of facticity. Everything can be conceived of as contingent, depending on human tropism, everything except contingency itself. Contingency, and only contingency, is absolutely necessary: facticity, and only facticity, is not factual, but eternal. Facticity is not a fact, it is not one more fact in the world. And this is based upon a precise argument: I can't be skeptical towards the operator for every skepticism. This necessity of facticity, this non-facticity of the facticity, I call in French the "factualité" – that is, in Ray Brassier's translation, "factiality". Factiality is not facticity, but the necessity of facticity, the essence of facticity. And the principle which enounces the factiality, I simply call "the principle of factiality". Finally, I call "spéculation factuale", "factial speculation", the speculation grounded on the principle of factiality. Through the principle of factiality, I maintain that I can attain a speculative materialism which clearly refutes correlationism. I can think an X independent of any thinking: and I know this, thanks to the correlationist himself and his fight against the absolute. The principle of factiality unveils the ontological truth hidden beneath the radical skepticism of modern philosophy, to be is not to be a correlate, but to be a fact, to be is to be factual, and this is not a fact.

4. *The principle of contradiction*

Now, what can we say about this absolute which is identified with facticity? What is facticity once it is considered as an absolute rather than as a limit? The answer is *time*. Facticity as absolute must be considered as time, *but a very special time*, that I called in *After Finitude* "hyper-chaos". What do I mean by this term? To say that the absolute is time, or chaos, seems very trite, very banal. But the time we discover here is, as I said, a very special time: not a physical time, not an ordinary chaos. Hyper-chaos is very different from what we call usually "chaos". By chaos we usually mean disorder, randomness, the eternal becoming of everything. But these properties are not properties of Hyper-Chaos: its contingency is so radical that even becoming, disorder, or randomness can be destroyed by it, and replaced by order, determinism, and fixity. Things are so contingent in Hyper-chaos, that time is able to destroy even the becoming of things. If facticity is the absolute, contingency no longer means the necessity of destruction or disorder, but rather the equal contingency of order and disorder, of becoming and sempiternity. That's why I now prefer to use the terms "surcontingence", "supercontingency", rather than contingency. We must understand that this thesis about time is very different from Heraclitus' philosophy: Heraclitus, according to me, is a terrible fixist. His becoming must become, and persist eternally as becoming. Why? This is, according to me, a dogmatic assessment, without any justification: because, according to me becoming is just a fact – as well as fixity – and so becoming and fixity must both have the eternal possibility to appear and disappear. But Heraclitean becoming is also, like all physical time, governed by specific laws, laws of transformation which never change. But there is no reason why a physical law endures, or persists, one more day, one more minute. Because these laws are just facts: you can't demonstrate their necessity. Hume demonstrated this point very clearly. But this impossibility of demonstrating the necessity of physical laws is not, according to me, due to the limits of reason, as Hume believed, but rather due to the fact that it is just *false*. I'm a rationalist, and reason clearly demonstrates that you can't demonstrate necessity of laws. Thus we should just believe reason and accept this point: laws are not necessary, they are facts, and facts are contingent, they can change without reason. Time is not governed by physical laws because it is the laws themselves which are governed by a mad time.

Here, I'd like to emphasize the type of rupture which I try to introduce with regard to both principal modalities of metaphysics: "the metaphysics of substance" and "the metaphysics of becoming". I believe that the opposition between being (conceived as substrate) and becoming is included in the principle of reason, which is the operator of every metaphysics. This is the sense of the initial opposition in the Presocratics, between Thales – who is a thinker of the *archè* conceived of as substrate, i.e. water – and Anaximander – who is a thinker of the *archè* as *apeiron*, which is to say the necessary becoming and destruction of every entity. Thinkers of becoming such as Heraclitus, Nietzsche, or Deleuze, are often considered as antimetaphysicians, as metaphysics is considered as the philosophy of fixed principles, such as substances and Ideas. But metaphysics is in fact defined by its belief in the determinate necessity of entities or of processes: things must be what they are, or must become what they become because there is a reason for this (for example the Idea, or the Creativity of Universe). That is why metaphysics of becoming believe in two metaphysical necessities: the necessity of becoming, rather than of fixity; and the necessity of such and such a becoming, rather than of others that are equally thinkable. On the contrary, the notion of Hyper-Chaos is the idea of a time so completely liberated from metaphysical necessity that nothing constrains it: neither becoming, nor the substratum. This hyper-chaotic time is able to create and destroy even becoming, producing without reason fixity or movement, repetition or creation. That's why I think that ultimately the matter of philosophy is not being or becoming, representation or reality, but a very special possibility, which is not a formal possible, but a real and dense possible, which I call the "peut-être", the "may-be". In French, I would say: "l'affaire de la philosophie n'est pas l'être, mais le peut-être". Philosophy's main concern is not with being but with the may-be. This *peut-être*, I believe, but it would be too complex to demonstrate this here, is very close to the final *peut-être* of Mallarmé's *Un Coup de dés*.

If facticity is the absolute, then facticity must be thought as hyper-chaos, a rationalist chaos that is paradoxically more chaotic than any antirationalist chaos. But even if we accept this point, it seems we have a serious problem: how can we hope to resolve the problem of ancestrality with such a notion? This problem, indeed, consisted in discovering an absolute capable of founding the legitimacy of a scientific knowledge of the reality in itself. We now have an absolute that is, I believe, able to resist correlationism, but this absolute seems to be the contrary of a rational structure of being: it is the destruction of the principle of reason, through which we try to explain the reason for facts. Now, it seems, there are only facts, and no more reason. How can we hope to ground the sciences with such a result? I think there is a way to resolve this new problem. How could we do it? My thesis is that there are specific conditions of facticity, which I call "figures": I mean, facticity is for me the only necessity of things but to be factual implies not to be just anything. To be factual is not given just to any sort of thing. Some things, if they existed, wouldn't obey the strict and necessary conditions for being a factual entity. That's why these things can't exist: they can't exist, because if they existed, they would be necessary, and to be necessary, according to the principle of factiality, is impossible. Let's give an example. I try to show, in *After Finitude*, that non-contradiction is a condition of contingency, for a contradictory reality couldn't change since it would already be what it is not. More precisely, imagine or rather try to conceive of what a being able to support any contradiction would be: it has the property a, and at the same time, and in exactly the same conditions it has the property not-a. The object is only red, and not only red but also non-red. And it is the same for any property you can conceive of: b and not-b, c and not-c, etc. Now, try to conceive that this entity has to change, to become something it is not, would it be conceivable? Of course not, it is already everything and its contrary. A contradictory being is perfectly necessary. That is why the Christian God is at once what he is – the Father, infinite, eternal – and what he is not – the Son, human, and mortal. If you want to think something necessary, you have to think it as contradictory, without any alterity, with nothing outside the absolute that the absolute could become. This is also ultimately why the Hegelian absolute is effectively contradictory: because Hegel understood that a being that is really necessary, such as an absolute, would have to be what it is and what it is not, it would have to have already inside itself what is outside of it. Such an absolute would have no alterity, and hence would be eternal (but this of course would be a contradictory eternity which doesn't have becoming outside itself, which has within itself an eternal becoming eternally passing in to eternity).

On the contrary, I maintain that contradiction is impossible – that's why I'm a rationalist – but I maintain that it is impossible because non-contradiction is the condition of a radical Chaos, that is, a Hyper-Chaos. Notice that I don't claim that a contradictory being is impossible, because it is absurd, or because it is non-sense. On the contrary, I think that a contradictory being is not meaningless: you can define it rigourously, and you can reason about it. You can rationally demonstrate that a real contradiction is impossible because it would be a necessary being. In others words, it is because the metaphysical principle of reason is absolutely false, that the logical principle of non-contradiction is absolutely true. The perfect "logicity" of everything is a strict condition of the absolute absence of reason for anything. That's why I don't believe in metaphysics in general: because a metaphysics always believes, in one way or the other, in the principle of reason. A metaphysician is a philosopher who believes it is possible to explain why things must be what they are, or why things must necessarily change, and perish, or why things must change as they do change. I believe on the contrary that reason has to explain why things and why becoming itself can always become what they are not, and why there is no ultimate reason for this game. In this way, "factial speculation" is still a form of rationalism, but a paradoxical one: it is a rationalism which explains why things must be without reason, and how precisely they can be without reason. Figures are such necessary modalities of facticity, and non-contradiction is the first figure I deduce from the principle of factiality. This demonstrates that one can reason about the absence of reason, if the very idea of reason is subjected to a profound transformation, if it becomes a reason liberated from the principle of reason, or, more exactly, if it is a reason which liberates us from principle of reason.

Now, my project is to solve a problem that I did not resolve in *After Finitude*, it is a very difficult problem, one that I can't rigorously set out here, but that I can sum up in this simple question: would it be possible to derive, to draw from the principle of factiality, the ability of the natural sciences to know, by way of mathematical discourse, reality in itself, by which I mean our world, the factual world as it is actually produced by Hyper-chaos, and which exists independently of our subjectivity? To answer this very difficult problem is a condition for a real resolution of the problem of ancestrality, and this constitutes the theoretical finality of my present work.

Anna Longo

THE CONTINGENT EMERGENCE OF THOUGHT

A comparison between Meillassoux and Deleuze

1. Speculative Realism and Speculative Materialism

"Time without becoming" is the text of a lecture Quentin Meillassoux gave at the Middlesex University in May 2008. At that time, he made a summary of the arguments he employed in *After Finitude*[1] to overcome the correlation from the inside and to rationally access the absolute: the contingency of everything that can be. His effort to reach the absolute after centuries of critical limitation has been considered a part of a more general philosophical turn: "Speculative Realism". This expression was first used as the title for a workshop that took place in April 2007 at Goldsmiths, University of London, where Ray Brassier, Iain Hamilton Grant, Graham Harman and, of course, Quentin Meillassoux discussed their anti-correlationist strategies in a public debate. This event had large resonance and it brought about a wider wave of speculative realisms involving an increasing number of thinkers and scholars all over the world. However, rather than constituting an homogeneous movement or school, Speculative Realism must be considered as an "umbrella term" for very different philosophical approaches that share a common enemy: correlationism. This is the reason why the protagonists of this speculative turn are today stressing the originality of their personal approaches by underlining their reciprocal incompatibilities. This is the case of Meillasoux, who defines his own philosophy as "Speculative Materialism" rather than "Speculative Realism" in order to distance

---

1   Q. Meillassoux, *After Finitude*, New York: Continuum 2004.

himself from the rest of group. As he has explained[2], his own materialist project consists not only in overcoming correlationism to access a non dogmatic absolute, but also in avoiding what he calls "Subjectalism"[3], a strategy of absolutization of the correlational circle, that is, of an aspect of the subject/object relation. According to Meillassoux, in fact, at least two of the participants in Speculative Realism, are subjectalists rather than materialists, as they access a real that is in fact the hypostatization of some feature of the subjective experience of the world. To be a materialist, on the contrary, means to access things as a total exteriority, to access them as completely different from the living intelligent subject. This materialist assumption entails an original solution to the question of the genesis of the transcendental, i.e. of the genesis of thought.

In this contribution I will focus on this specific issue. I will try to follow Meillassoux's arguments concerning this impressive solution to the problem of the genesis of intelligent life. I will then compare his argument to Deleuze's transcendental empiricism in order to understand if it may actually constitute a kind of subjectalism and what the reasons would be for refusing Meillassoux's materialist position.

---

2   Q. Meillassoux, *Iteration, Reiteration, Repetition: a Speculative Analysis of the Meaningless Sign,* Freie Universität, 20th April 2012, text available on-line at: http://cdn.shopify.com/s/files/1/0069/6232/files/Meillassoux_Workshop_Berlin.pdf

3   In "Time without becoming" Meillassoux is still using the term "subjectivism" to refer to philosophies that extend one more character of the subject to being in general. The term has been substituted by "subjectalism" more recently, as can be seen in the text of conference "Iteration, Reiteration, Repetition: a speculative analysis of the meaningless sign".

2. *The reciprocal exteriority of inorganic matter and intelligent life*

Meillassoux defines his philosophy as "Speculative Materialism" rather than "Speculative Realism" since he aims not only to overcome correlationism but also *subjectalism*, which, according to him, consists in hypostatizing one of the subject's properties like life, reason, sensibility, agency, etc. This double aim would differentiate his philosophical project from those of other speculative realists, such as Graham Harman and Iain Hamilton Grant, who, according to him, are anti-correlationist but subjectalist. Harman, in fact, hypostatizes the human subject's sensible relation to objects by generalizing it: any object is in a phenomenological relation with all the other objects, so the essence of any object is hidden while sensible qualities are manifest to all other objects. In this way he can claim that the way of being of any object is through its withdrawal from any relation, while manifesting itself through perceivable qualities or features. For Harman, the reason why we cannot know things in themselves is that things in themselves withdraw behind their appearance and that withdrawal constitutes the truth about any object. It is not our knowledge that is limited, but it is the limitation of knowledge that constitues a positive truth about any object: they are not as they manifest themselves; they withdraw from any relation while they are perceived as withdrawn from any relation. Instead Grant, following Shelling, states that the absolute is nature's creative and free production, a process driven by nature's ideas as immanent tendencies. These can be grasped as something that exceeds their conception since they are the determinant condition of concepts: thought does not think nature's ideas but according to them, so that thinking is part of natural production, an expression of its freedom. Thus, thought would know the process as its own being and as the being of everything: the relation between thought and the real would be a kind of self-representation of nature to itself, which would exclude the existence of unknowable things in-themselves beyond the necessary correlation. In both cases, in Harman as well as in Grant, a particular feature of the subject's relation to the world, such as the phenomenological perception or free productivity, is acknowledged as the necessary feature of all beings, living or dead. This entails that the inorganic cannot be considered as totally exterior, but rather that it is meant to depend on the internal features that are hypostatized in the subject. From this standpoint, objects are not determined by the subject according to her unique a priori structure, but it is the a priori structure that is determined by the real as a necessary and essential feature that guarantees the veracity of the subjective relation to the world. The real, as it is in itself, is the reason why it is in a certain way for us, the reason for the subject's correlation to it; and the limits of our knowledge are turned into the truth about the real condition for the existence of understanding. In fact, Harman states that there is nothing more to know about objects than the fact that they manifest their withdrawal, that they are not what they appear; while Grant claims that there is nothing more to know besides the way in which the process produces a representation of itself through thought, so that the real is the correlate of thought as its prior condition. Thus, for Meillassoux, these two realisms can be considered two forms of subjectalism: both consist in the absolutization of a special feature of the correlation and they make the limits of knowledge into a positive aspect of the in it-self. In is this way the subjective property that is hypostatized – like thought, life, sensibility, creativity, will, etc. – actually determines the knowledge the in it-self as that which renders the correlation necessary. We find this kind of reasoning in Hegel, for example, where thought knows objects as exteriorizations of itself and so it discovers to be the determinant of its own knowledge: there is nothing beyond the correlation between thought and the real since thought is the real. According to Meillassoux, we can find the same subjectalist approach, among others, in Nietzsche's vitalism, where the will to power is the underlying force of becoming that knows itself as itself wanting becoming. The subject's will to know is merely the means by which life knows its own purposeless productivity. For the same reason, also Deleuze's philosophy, inspired as it is by Nietzsche and Bergson, would be a kind of subjectalism where difference is the being of a becoming that knows itself as difference, a creation, as a proliferation of simulacra. Since subjectalist systems claim that it is possible to access the last instance of the real as life, will, thought, creativity, freedom, etc., they can be considered as realist rather than as correlationist philosophies, but they are not materialisms since they do not assume the reciprocal exteriority between subject and object, between thought and things. In subjectalist systems, one of the properties of the living intelligent subject is always considered to be a feature of everything, of the organic as well as of the inorganic. On the contrary, being materialist, and specifically a speculative materialist like Meillassoux, implies to assume that there is a rational access to the inorganic in itself, without projecting onto it any subjective property. It means to know the inorganic as it was before the emergence of intelligent life, as something that is completely independent from the subject's relation to it, and as such the inorganic cannot be considered as the condition for the production of intelligent life. Ultimately, this implies that intelligent life cannot be considered as a necessary, or at least a possible, production of the inorganic, since in this case it would be contained as a potentiality in dead matter, which would be, in a certain way, already living and intelligent. If the inorganic were the condition for the emergence of intelligent life, then intelligent life would know the inorganic as potential intelligent life rather than as a completely other, as completely different, indifferent and independent. If the inorganic were the condition for the emergence of intelligent life, then intelligent life would be a kind of production of the inorganic's self-consciousness, in an absolute idealistic fashion. This is the reason why Meillassoux disagrees with Hegel's Idealism, as well as with all vitalisms and with some of his colleagues' positions, even though their approaches are actually realist anticorrelationisms. Meillaussoux's goal is to demonstrate that reason is not only able to know the in it-self but also to know it as completely heterogeneous and totally independent: thought can know dead matter as something with which it shares nothing, not an origin, nor the condition of its being. In other words, Meillassoux's materialist claim is not only that knowledge of the real as an independent subject is possible, but that this knowledge is a knowledge of the independent emergence of intelligent life, an event whose conditions were not already given in the inorganic.

At this point it would be clear that the rational access to the contingency of any possible fact offers a solution to this problem: since everything is contingent then the emergence of intelligent life also happened without a reason, it constitutes an actualization whose conditions are determined by any potentiality already present in the inorganic. It seems to me that this point is extremely important in order to understand the specificity of Meillassoux's materialist position, since what actually differentiates him from many other realists is this explanation of the genesis of the transcendental as a fact that is not determined by the laws of the inorganic. The only condition of thought, which is the condition of the existence of everything, is the necessity of contingency: it is because anything must be contingent that thought and dead matter can be thought as not sharing anything; it is because everything is contingent that thought can know the inorganic as something that is totally exterior and independent.

3. *The contingent genesis of the transcendental*

The absolute contingency of everything is the conclusion of a very subtle argument that uses correlationists' anti-absolutism against idealism and vitalism in order to overcome the limits of the correlation itself. It is important to notice that the existence of a transcendental is not denied, but the a-priori of reason, in this case mathematics' set theory, is understood to be able to access an absolute property of everything that can be: its contingency. In fact, for Meillassoux, Kant's mistake did not consist in having established a rational a-priori allowing objective representation, but in thinking that it could not be used to access the in-itself; and the reason for this mistake was that Kant believed that natural laws were necessary, even if he was not able to prove it. In other words, Kant did not realize that contingent laws do not have to change continuously, that they can be stable, so he could not accept their contingency which for him implied the impossibility of representation. In fact, when dealing with Hume's problem of induction in his *Transcendental Deduction*, Kant states that laws cannot be contingent since, if that would be the case, everything would change so frequently that representation would be impossible. According to Meillassoux, on the contrary, contingent laws do not have to change frequently; if they were obliged to change frequently we would have to suppose a reason for their instability, so we would have to assume the existence of a necessary chaos, that implies a necessary becoming rather than a contingent order (that eventually could be substituted by a chaotic becoming which has no reason to persist). Thus, to Meillassoux, the only mistake in Kant's correlationism consists in not having taken into account that the impossibility of demonstrating the necessity of the laws is not a proof of the limitation of our understanding, but it is the evidence that they are actually without necessity. Accordingly, correlationism, which is a form of rationalism, actually had the power to reach the absolute but it was prevented to do this by the wrong conviction that the observed stability of the laws needed a reason. As Meillassoux explains, the contingency of the laws does not render representation impossible, since contingent laws can happen to be stable: they do not have a reason to persist but they do not have a reason to change frequently. Moreover, scientific mathematical formalizations of the laws of our stable world do not need to assume their necessity. From a logical point of view, in fact, mathematical functions are non-necessary: one function and its opposite are both thinkable as possible and there is no reason to claim that one must be actualized rather than the other. Rationality allows us to imagine many different worlds, governed by very different laws, without forcing us to think of a reason for some functions to be actualized in lieu of others that are equally conceivable: it is absolutely logical to think that the functions representing laws are contingent. Thus, that laws are contingent is a conclusion that actually justifies scientific knowledge and its mathematical representations of the facts that we experience in this contingently stable world. Furthermore, it is because facts are contingent that they can be mathematically described, since only non-contradictory facts can be formalized. So the conclusion that natural laws are contingent is totally compatible with scientific knowledge, which is knowledge of the inorganic as independent from any subject – mathematical representation considers only primary qualities, i.e. quantities that must be considered independent of subjective perception. Science is thus able to know the inorganic as an exteriority independent from the subject, deprived of any character of life such as intelligence, sensibility or purposefulness. The inorganic is known as a dead mechanism moved by quantifiable forces instead of being the condition for the emergence of intelligent life, as is the case in a teleological perspective. Therefore, ancestrality is not only a reality preceding the event of intelligent life, but it is also a reality that cannot be conceived as the condition of the emergence of subjectivity. If that was the case, we would find the unexpressed potentiality of the organic, and thus of the correlation itself, in the inorganic, so there that there would be no reciprocal independence between dead matter and subjective life. Meillassoux thus dismisses the hypothesis that the potentiality for the emergence of intelligent life was already contained in the inorganic, and for similar reasons he equally refuses the idea that intelligent life is an unpredictable product of chance. As we read in his article "Potentiality and Virtuality" [4], this idea must be excluded because the notion of chance implies an already given totality of possibilities that, in this case, cannot be actually known, which is the reason why the probability of the event of the emergence of intelligent life cannot be predicted. The hazardous event of the emergence intelligent life would be the actualization of a possibility already given in a totality of possibilities that we cannot grasp as a whole, that the unpredictability of the event would constitute merely the correlate of our ignorance, as we are not able to think the necessary All. Thus, thinking that intelligent life is an event that happened by chance is just "the correlate of the unthinkability of the All" [5]: the fact is considered to be irreducible to its conditions because of our incapacity to discern the inner potentiality in the situation that precedes the emergence.

Thus, Meillassoux's demonstration of the contingency of laws can be used to dismiss common assumptions about the emergence of intelligent life, since they suppose that the potentiality of intelligent life was already given in an unthinkable original All. In fact, if anything must be contingent, then the original All is not unthinkable but actually non-existent: it would be necessary and contradictory. Moreover, according to Meillassoux, set theory clearly states that the set of all rationally determinable laws of nature, as mathematical functions, does not constitute a totality but an untotalizable set, and this implies that in this case we cannot apply the probability calculus. From this standpoint, the conditions for the emergence of life and thought were not already given within the set of laws that preceded their apparition. They emerged instead in an absolutely contingent way – out of

---

4   Q. Meillassoux, "Potentiality and virtuality", in *Collapse II*: Speculative Realism, March 2007, p. 55 – 81.

5   "We can then challenge the irrationalism that typically accompanies the affirmation of a novelty irreducible to the elements of the situation within which it occurs, since such an emergence becomes, on the contrary, the correlate of the rational unthinkability of the All". Q. Meillassoux, "Potentiality and Virtuality", ibid., p. 80.

nothing – so they cannot even be considered to be products of chance (that implies an already given totality), but real novelties, an outcome that happens without any reason. Life and thought are contingent facts that happened according to the non-necessity of laws, rather than according to some already given potentiality: they are non-necessary actualizations independent from any already given condition.

Meillassoux calls it *Hyper-chaos* the virtual, untotalizable set of the possible functions that can be actualized as natural laws for any possible world. It differs from the necessary All of metaphysics since it is not an already given totality of possibilities and, as a consequence, the probability of its actualizations cannot be calculated in advance, as we do when we think of the chance of an event that is already determined as possible. Hyper-chaos actualizes facts which are unpredictable not because of our limited understanding of the totality of the All, but because they do not have any reason nor even probability, to be actualized. Actualizations of the virtual Hyper-chaos are absolutely independent of any previous situation, i.e. they are emergences whose condition is contingency itself. Thus, it is only by admitting that laws governing the inorganic are contingent that Meillassoux can justify the emergence of intelligent life as something which is totally independent from the inorganic, and from any necessary reason that would contain its potentiality. Accordingly, not only the inorganic can be considered as an exteriority independent from the subject, but also the fact the subject's existence can be considered as totally independent from the existence of dead matter. In other words, intelligent life can be considered an actual novelty that emerged *ex-nihilo* within a context of non-necessary natural laws that cannot be considered as responsible for its production, under the guise of its necessary conditions. This reciprocal exteriority of the inorganic and the organic renders materialism actually possible. Moreover, this exteriority is clearly accessible by reason: it is absolutely rational to admit the contingency of laws and, thus, the absolute contingency of the emergence of life and thought. We do not need to look for the cause of their actualization in dead matter nor in an already given metaphysical totality of possibilities. This entails that it is rational to assume that the inorganic can be known as independent from the subject, as something that does not need to be considered as the condition for the determination of thought. This argument excludes idealistic and vitalistic approaches according to which there is an underlying necessary force, or entity, that determines the production of thought and things as correlates. Thus the rational and positive knowledge of the necessity of the contingency of natural laws eliminates the possibility of thinking the world as a necessary process where the inorganic becomes conscious of itself through its necessary productions. This process of becoming would render thought a necessary emergence rather than a contingent fact deprived of reason.

What must be explained, at this point, is why Mellasissoux claims that the virtual Hyper-chaos is time. Since the contingent facts that can be actualized must be non contradictory in order to be mathematically representable, then it is impossible for two contradictory facts to be actualized at the same time or for one fact to become its opposite (in this case it would be already its contrary, which would make it contradictory). This implies that there must be a temporal succession for actualizations: if they are not logically coherent, then one fact can only emerge after the destruction of a previous one. So, given that we have a world provided with its own set of mathematical laws, this world can experience the change of its laws or the emergence of new laws (like the emergence of intelligent life within the ancestral world of the inorganic), but it must be destroyed before the actualization of a world which is its opposite. Meillassoux's contingent changes do not happen within a unique process of becoming, but one after the other, in a temporal succession. Hyper-chaos is the time within which the series of virtually possible contingent facts are actualized and destroyed without a reason; it is not the eternal All of the possible becomings of an already given set of potentialities. Hyper-chaos, then, is a rational chaos whose actualizations can be mathematically described since they are non-contradictory, and this is why science is able to describe our world in a subject-independent way, as if there were no living beings and no subjects in it. The rationality of facts does not depend on the subject but on the necessary contingency of everything that can be. This entails that reason can know its own contingency, it can conceive of itself as a contingent fact that has no reason to be and that happens to be able to provide a mathematical description of the other contingent facts as totally exterior and independent.

It is clear that, by rationally accessing the contingency of everything and the contingency of the fact of the existence of intelligent life, Meillassoux offers an answer to the problem of the genesis of the transcendental that avoids to make of the inorganic and the organic the products of an immanent necessary force, or of an All of potentialities, as it happens with idealism and vitalism. Thus Meillassoux's Speculative Materialism can be understood as a solution for justifying the being of the correlation, in this case the idea that the real can be represented thanks to the a-priori of mathematics, without admitting any metaphysical necessary reason and without claiming that such reason is beyond the limits of our understanding. In this way correlationism is overcome, since Meillassoux demonstrates that the rational transcendental can actually access the absolute beyond the limits of experience (the contingency of everything). However, we have to notice that this strategy does not consist in dismissing the idea that there is a logical a-priori that allows representation, but in increasing its power. Mathematics is actually the a-priori that permits the description of the real as independent from the subject, and that allows the understanding that contingency is a necessary ontological property of being. Moreover, not only the mathematical a-priori, which happened to be actualized without a reason, can be used to know the present world of our experience, but also to access the ancestral inexperienced past and to describe the virtually possible worlds that might be actualized by the Hyper-chaos. In other words, Meillassoux legitimizes the use of the mathematical transcendental beyond the limits of experience and, at the same time, he offers a rational answer to the question of the genesis of the transcendental: thought is a contingent fact that happened without a reason like all other contingent facts, and this is why it is able to represent them independently from the subject's sensible experience.

4. *Deleuze's becoming without time*

According to Meillassoux, Deleuze's philosophy is a kind of vitalism or subjectalism, since thought is supposed to be determined by the real as a production that is part of a real process of differentiation, and of becoming. For Deleuze, thinking would be a way of taking part in the becoming of everything, and the real would be known as the variable condition for the creation of concepts in thought. Then, thought would access the real as the virtual problem that it solves by producing concepts, and knowledge would consists in grasping the differentiating conditions for philosophical creation. Knowing would be a way of taking part in the becoming determined by the real. In this sense there would be a kind of circularity that can be said to be an absolutization of the correlation, since a property of the subject's relation to things, in this case differentiating creativity, is considered to be an essential property of the real and the reason for the determination of the transcendental, i.e. of the correlation. This implies that thought accesses the real as its own condition of differentiation rather than as an independent exteriority. It is for this reason that for Meillassoux, Deleuze's transcendental empiricism is not a genuine form of materialism but a kind of idealism where the correlation between thought and things is determined by a necessary process that is actually the real, the being of becoming.

However it seems to me that Deleuze's anti-Kantianism must be taken into account, since his objections to criticism are valid to challenge also Meillassoux's materialist position. What Deleuze did not accept is the idea that the possible experience can be determined a-priori by a given invariable a-priori logical structure, such as assuming that the real has to be necessarily rational and non-contradictory. In other words, he believed that the transcendental structure is not eternal but that it changes according to the stimulation of a real irrational becoming. To this regard, we have to consider that for Meillassoux the mathematics of set theory must be considered as a rational given a-priori that is supposed to be valid in itself: it cannot change, and it is the only fact that we have to trust in order to obtain a correct representation of facts. Thus, for Meillassoux, rationality, as it has been contingently actualized, is endowed with precise stable rules and its principle is non-contradiction: to think correctly we have to follow this rational a-priori. In fact, it is following the rules of rationality that Meillassoux accesses the absolute contingency of everything, which implies that only non-contradictory facts can be actualized. But in this way he is turning a rational principle (non-contradiction) into an ontological principle and this means that he is considering that the possible is already determined a-priori according to the identity of a rational transcendental: anything can be rationally determined in advance, before its actualization, since anything is supposed to be rationally representable (what is not rationally representable cannot happen). And this is exactly the idea against which Deleuze elaborates his philosophy, the notion that there is a given transcendental which cannot evolve according to the evolution of a real that is erroneously considered to be already determined by rational laws, like non-contradiction. In other words, for Deleuze, it is a mistake to think that the real must respect the a-priori of rationality and that nothing "irrational" can happen which forces thought to change, to evolve, to re-create its rules. Deleuze's point of departure, in fact, is the creativity of thought, and he aims at explaining the evidence for the historical becoming of philosophy. According to him, Kant's stable transcendental prevents philosophical creation, as it consists in the application of the same rules and in the exclusion of the possibility that the experience of the real can bring something new, forcing thought to change. According to Deleuze, Kant's image of thought, which is very similar to Meillassoux's in terms of stability, must be overturned, since it does not allow to grasp the essentially irrational becoming of the real, its productivity, and its capacity for determining the evolution of thinking. To him, in fact, the real is able to produce the contradictory, to change its own rules in a way that cannot be established a-priori by a fixed rational transcendental. Thus, to Deleuze, Kant's and Meillassoux's philosophies are illegitimate ways of subordinating the real differences to a supposed identity of thought by constructing a dead, invariable and consensual image of it. Moreover, Deleuze would recognize in Meillassoux's materialism another problem: it assumes to know the inorganic as a dead independent exteriority and thought as a dead axiomatic, but it is not able to understand life. So it is actually the separation between thought, as system of representation, and being, as represented, that Deleuze wants to challenge in order to understand how thought can be forced by real intensities to create new rules, to evolve, to change.

Thus, the disagreement between Meillassoux and Deleuze concerns exactly the issue of the genesis of the transcendental and the meaning of "thinking". For Meillassoux thinking is following the rational transcendental in order to reach the absolute by demonstrating that the logical principle of non-contradiction is an ontological principle and not just a rule of representation. On the contrary, for Deleuze it is a matter of extending the principle of reason to the abolition of the logical principle of non-contradiction by showing that thinking means to create new concepts and to invent new rules according to the irrational contradictory becoming of the real. Thus for Meillassoux, Deleuze is not following rationality – since he admits the existence of a contradictory

necessary being of becoming that cannot be known as a fact
independent from the subject but only as the condition for
thinking. On the contrary, for Deleuze, Meillassoux is erroneously considering that a rational principle, such as non-
contradiction, is an ontological principle and in this way he
is preventing himself from the possibility of grasping the inner creativity of the real and of thought. So for the former
thinking means to apply the given rational transcendental
to be able to access the absolute rationality of everything
that can be, and for the latter thinking means to change the
given rules of thought according to the creativity of a real
that is the reason for the irrational becoming of everything
and of the transcedental. From this opposition in the conception of the meaning of thinking derives the difference
between Meillassoux's and Deleuze's notions of the virtual.
For the younger philosopher, the virtual is like a dice with
an untotalizable number of faces that is thrown in a temporal succession: at any throw a contingent fact is substituted
by another one and any outcome is non-contradictory and
mathematically representable. This game of dice is subjected
to a major rule, the rational principle of non-contradiction,
according to which only contingent facts can happen without
a reason and any fact can be mathematically represented. On
the contrary, for Deleuze the virtual is the eternal already
given time, Aion, that can be divided infinitely, it is the
unique throw of dice that is divided in an untotalizable set
of throws. Like in Borges' lottery[6], any throw of dice implies
other throws that decide for the alternatives that are opened
by the previous one. For example, the outcome of a sentence,
decided by a throw of dice, implies other throws to choose
the modality of the punishment, the option between prison
and death, the modality of the death, ad infinitum. In this
way, any outcome does not cease to imply an infinity of dif-
ferentiations, an infinity of other outcomes, all subdivision

---

6   Jorge Luis Borges, "The Lottery in Babylon", in *Ficciones*, New
     York: Grove Press 1962.

of the first one. Thus, Deleuze's virtual, as an already given finite eternity, is the throw that affirms, in one gesture, all the diverging series of contradictory ramifications of chance. It is a becoming without time rather than time without becoming. Moreover, in this way the alternatives of the disjunctions, that according to the principle of non-contradiction cannot exists at the same time, are affirmed in an irrational and chaotic disjunctive synthesis. If in Meillassoux's game of dice thinking means to represent rationally representable outcomes, in Deleuze thinking means to throw the dice one more time in order to complicate the series, in order to actualize a new rule. For Deleuze, thinking finds its condition of being in the series of all the previous throws that the thinker contributes to differentiate. In Meillassoux's game, on the contrary, thought is one of the possible outcome of the virtual and rational dice, where any throw actualizes a fact which is totally independent from the series of previous results. In Meillassoux thought is the outcome that can represent all the other possible non-contradictory outcomes, since the whole game has a rule that happened to be the rule of thinking. For Deleuze, the thinker takes part in an irrational game whose rules are always changing, and her intervention produces a new change whose conditions are already established within the series that she contributes to ramify.

In order to conclude, I do not want to endorse one position against the other, but only to underline that the two conclusions derive from two very different assumptions: on one side Meillassoux trusts representation and he excludes that non-representable facts can happen, on the other side Deleuze trusts the real as being able to force thinking to constantly change the rules of representation. Meillasoux's rationalism arrives to establish that the logical principle of non-contradiction is an ontological principle. On the contrary, Deleuze's anti-rationalism arrives to establish that the principles of rationality are just the temporary results of a real irrational becoming. Thus if we want to justify why science is able to mathematically represent the inorganic as subject independent we find a good answer in Meillassoux, but if we want to understand why thought is able to reinvent its rules and to create new logics and systems we find a better answer in Deleuze. We still miss a philosophical system capable to explain, at the same time, why scientific knowledge is possible and why thought is able to re-create its own rules under the stimulation of the real.

I would like to thank Carlos Basualdo for reading and commenting the previous version of my text

MIMESIS GROUP
www.mimesis-group.com

MIMESIS INTERNATIONAL
www.mimesisinternational.com
info@mimesisinternational.com

MIMESIS EDIZIONI
www.mimesisedizioni.it
mimesis@mimesisedizioni.it

ÉDITIONS MIMÉSIS
www.editionsmimesis.fr
info@editionsmimesis.fr

MIMESIS AFRICA
www.mimesisafrica.com
info@mimesisafrica.com

MIMESIS COMMUNICATION
www.mim-c.net

MIMESIS EU
www.mim-eu.com

printed by Digital Team
Fano (PU) in July 2014